At the
RESTAURANT
Activity Book

Alice Hobbs

Illustrated by Putri Febriana

THIS BOOK BELONGS TO:

Ethan

QEB

·CONTENTS·

4   Let's go to the restaurant!

6   Who's the chef?

8   Let's go shopping

9   Dot-to-dot

10 Superfoods—true or false?

12 Number search

13 I spy game

14 Guess who?

16 Design time!

18 Shadow match

19 Untangle a maze of messy spaghetti

20 Spot the difference

22 Food critic

23 Create your dream pizza

24 Can you find?

26 The coolest new restaurant in town!

28 An alien invasion

30 What's wrong?

31 My dream meal

32 Good service

34 Where's my dinner?

36 Aware of the allergens!

37 Picnic in the park

38 Comic strip

40 Healthy eating

42 Milkshake mayhem

43 Recipe time!

44 National cuisine

46 Drawing lesson

48 Shapes and cakes

49 Wordsearch

50 Food journeys:
from farm to table

52 Color it in

54 Check, please!

55 Cookery competition

56 Maze

58 My meal at
the restaurant

60 Answers

LET'S GO TO THE RESTAURANT!

You and your family or friends want to go to a restaurant. Fill out this online booking form to reserve your table.

Your personal details and booking information can be true or made up.

- SUZI'S -
SUSHI BAR

Full name:

Phone number:

Address:

Number of people: Time:

Any special requirements:

MY FRIENDS

Kevin

Susi

James

Alice

Putri

Joanna

Fill out this invitation to invite whoever
you want to the restaurant with you.

Dear ....

You are invited to ....

At ....

From .... To ....

Dress code ....

Design the front
of the invitation. You
can use pens, pencils,
and crayons to draw
your design. Then
color it in.

Who's the chef?

There are many different restaurants and staff who work in them. Draw a line to match the chef to their restaurant. Once you've matched the chef to their restaurant, write the tastiest dish on their menu in the speech bubble.

Let's go shopping

Imagine you are a chef about to make a delicious bowl of ramen. Below is a list of some of the ingredients you need to make the noodle soup. Draw them in your shopping bag.

- ☐ Noodles
- ☐ One chili
- ☐ Six eggs
- ☐ Spring onions
- ☐ Mushrooms
- ☐ Two carrots

Dot-to-dot

Connect the dots to reveal what you're having for dessert. When you're finished, you can color it in.

SUPERFOODS-TRUE OR FALSE?

Here are some super-cool facts about food and healthy eating. But are they all true? Tick either true or false.

Superfoods are foods that have a very large amount of nutrients in them, and are super good for you!

1. If you eat lots of carrots, you will be able to see in the dark.

True	False
☐	☐

Lots of different foods can be classed as superfoods, including: fruits, vegetables, nuts, seeds, grains, fish, eggs, and more.

2. Bananas are actually berries.

True	False
☐	☐

3. Avocados grow in pairs.

True	False
☐	☐

4. Some varieties of corn are multicolored.

True ☐ False ☐

5. Frozen vegetables are less nutritious than fresh vegetables.

MIXED VEGETABLES

True ☐ False ☐

6. Oranges contain more vitamin C than broccoli.

True ☐ False ☐

Eating a range of superfoods can keep your immune system strong and healthy.

How many questions did you answer correctly? Check in the answers section and then see what your healthy eating knowledge rating is!

0–2 correct: Super

2–4 correct: Super-smart

4–6 correct: Superfoods superhero

Number search

The restaurant's order numbers are all mixed up. Help find them in the grid below so the customers can get their meals. The numbers may be forward, backward, up, down, or diagonal. Circle or highlight the numbers as you find them in the grid.

9	6	6	8	7	7	9	4
4	3	4	5	6	4	7	9
8	7	5	8	1	3	4	9
3	7	6	8	9	2	1	6
6	8	4	2	3	4	2	5
9	3	5	5	3	6	7	2
4	0	2	5	8	7	6	9
1	7	0	3	9	6	8	6

Order numbers

039	⬚	402	⬚	836	⬚
122	⬚	645	⬚	877	⬚
366	⬚	783	⬚	965	⬚

I SPY GAME

Can you spot these items or people in the restaurant?

1. A waiter
2. A menu
3. A fork
4. Flowers
5. Candles
6. A baby
7. A family having a meal
8. Some trainers
9. A glass of water
10. A handbag
11. A chef's hat
12. A hot drink
13. Something green
14. A dessert
15. A napkin

Guess who?

One of the people in the restaurant is a famous Olympic medalist. Follow the clues to find out who.

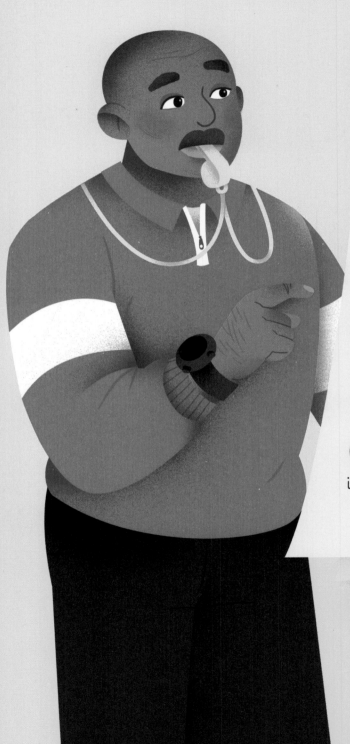

Cross out the people as you eliminate them and circle the Olympic medalist when you have found them.

Clue 1: They have a red top on

Clue 2: They have a bag by their feet

Clue 3: There is more than one other person at their table

Clue 4: They do not have brown hair

Clue 5: They have an empty plate in front of them

DeSign time!

A new restaurant is opening, and they have hired you to help design their uniforms and menu!

What is the name of this new restaurant? Design a logo.

Design the uniform for this new restaurant. Add colors, details, and a logo to the clothes below.

Design the front of your menu. Place your new logo here and add some decoration.

STARTERS

MAINS

DESSERTS

Now design the back and create a menu of your favorite dishes!

Shadow match

Draw a line between the item of food and its shadow. Below, write the name of the food.

1 ....

2 ....

3 ....

4 ....

5 ....

6 ....

18

UNTANGLE A MAZE OF MESSY SPAGHETTI

Follow the spaghetti strands to find your fork and untangle the messy pile of spaghetti! Draw the route using a pen or a pencil.

There are 10 differences to spot.

Food critic

Food critics sample and review food and write about their experiences in magazines and newspapers. Imagine you are a food critic for the day. In the space below, review your meal.

_____

_____

_____

_____

_____

_____

_____

_____

_____

_____

Create your dream pizza

Design your dream pizza below. You can draw on your favorite toppings, the best toppings ever, like chocolate buttons, or even the silliest, like snails. Then, color in your pizza toppings!

Can you find?

There are lots of staff working in this busy kitchen!
Can you find and circle these 12 kitchen items?

1. A glass
2. A wooden spoon
3. A chef's hat
4. A tomato
5. A bunch of grapes
6. A ladle
7. A bowl
8. A loaf of bread
9. An oven glove
10. A blue pair of pants
11. A pair of glasses
12. A clock

THE COOLEST NEW RESTAURANT IN TOWN!

Posters can be used to advertise restaurants and other attractions.

Which of these restaurants
would you like to go to best?

....

What would you order?

....

Create a poster to advertise a new restaurant opening in your local town. This could be your favorite restaurant, or something silly! Write the name of the restaurant and draw a picture of the restaurant or the food you can eat there.

An alien invasion

Fill in the blanks to complete the story. This game can be played alone, or with someone else. Follow the prompts and fill in the blanks to create a hilarious story. Once you've filled in all the blanks, read your story aloud. The funnier the words you choose, the sillier the story will be!

I was shocked and surprised when the lights in the restaurant all went

dark. I couldn't even see my _____.
(Meal)

There were _____ flashing lights and there
(Color)

was a strange smell of _____ in the air.
(Vegetable)

"Uh oh!" I exclaimed when an alien spaceship crashed through

the ceiling and landed on the floor of the restaurant.

Small aliens emerged from the ship eating _____.
(Type of candy)

They had _____ eyes and _____ legs.
(Number above 10)   (Number below 10)

Their faces looked like a _____ mixed with a _____.
(Type of fruit)   (Animal)

"Help!" I heard someone shout. I saw an alien standing in front of

_____. The alien said, _____.
(Name of family member)   (Made up word)

Then the alien pulled out _____
(Type of costume)

and some gold sunglasses, and told us to put them on.

Next, _____
(Favorite song)

started playing, the spaceship began spinning like a disco

ball, and the aliens started to _____.
(Dance move)

"Wow!" I cheered as everyone in the restaurant started dancing too.

"I never expected my evening at the restaurant to turn out like this!"

I thought as I danced my best moves.

What's wrong?

Candice is enjoying a birthday meal with her family for her 10th birthday. But there are some things wrong with the scene. Find and circle all eight things.

My dream meal

Design your dream meal. You can have whatever you want!
Draw a drink, main course, dessert, and side. Then, choose
some colors and color in the meal.

Use your pens and pencils to draw your favorite dessert here, the yummier the better!

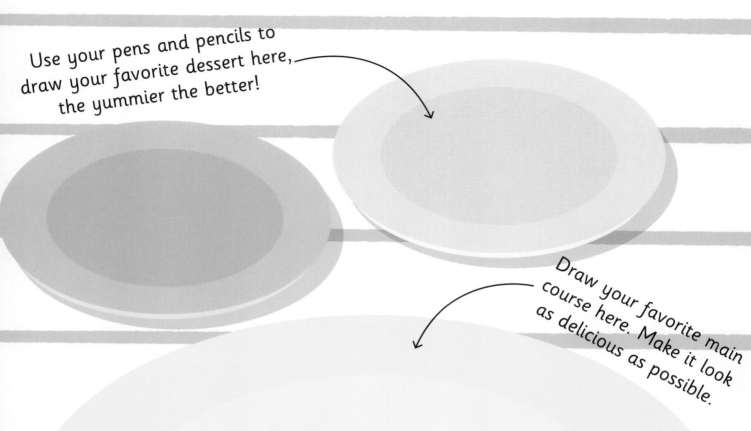

Draw your favorite main course here. Make it look as delicious as possible.

Good Service

Waiters need to be very alert to make sure everyone in the restaurant is happy and has what they need. Study this picture for three minutes. Then cover it and answer the questions on the opposite page from memory. No peeking!

How much can you remember from the picture?

1. Someone wants to order a meal. What color top are they wearing?

....

2. Is there a spill? What is it?

....

3. Something has been dropped on the floor. What is it?

....

4. The restaurant is busy tonight! How many people are seated?

....

5. Someone is taking bookings on the phone. What color hair do they have?

....

6. Guests are waiting to be seated. How many of them are there?

....

7. A waiter is carrying a meal to a table. What are they carrying?

....

WHERE'S MY DINNER?

Oh no! There is a holdup in the kitchen.
Look at each picture and write two short
stories about what has happened.

_____

_____

_____

_____

_____

_____

_____

Aware of the allergens!

Some people can't eat certain foods because they make them unwell—this is an allergy. Symbols like the ones below are used on menus to make sure people don't eat the food that they are allergic to.

Complete this symbol sudoku puzzle. Fill in each square with one of the symbols. Each symbol can appear only once in each row, column, and mini-grid.

Each symbol also has a number, so you can write the numbers instead, if you prefer.

1. Gluten
Gluten is found in wheat, and therefore foods like bread and pasta.

2. Sesame
A sesame allergy refers to sesame seeds.

3. Nuts
Nut allergies are among the most common food allergies.

4. Crustacean
Crustaceans are creatures with exoskeletons like crabs, lobsters, shrimp, and prawns.

Picnic in the park

Each picnic basket has a number below. Follow the dotted line to find out which picnic basket belongs to each family. Write the number below the picnic blanket.

1

2

3

comic Strip

Jamila has just been for a very special meal at the restaurant. In each box, draw what happened.

We arrived at the restaurant during a firework display.

When we sat down, the waiter brought over all our favorite food. The table was huge!

Next, a famous rock band performed
for us and all the other guests.

Then, a giant chocolate fountain was revealed for dessert.

Finally, a limousine arrived to collect us and drive us home.

Healthy eating

Nutritionists help people keep fit and healthy by encouraging them to eat all the foods their body needs.

Nadia the nutritionist has summarized the five different food groups below. Study the text before completing the activity on the next page.

Protein: This food group provides us with amino acids, which help our bodies repair themselves. Protein is found in meat and fish but also beans and pulses. These foods should make up only a small portion of our diet, one eighth.

Dairy and Dairy Alternatives: This is our main source of calcium. It is more important for children to have dairy in their diet, as it maintains healthy teeth and bones and is essential for growth. This should make up the second smallest portion of our diet.

Fats: Our body needs fats to survive, but we shouldn't eat too much fat. Fats help us to absorb vitamins, grow, and store energy. However, they should make up the smallest portion of our diets. Fat can be found in cakes and chips, but also in meat, fish, and vegetables.

Carbohydrates: Carbohydrates are our bodies' main source of energy. They also provide fiber, calcium, and iron. Lots of foods such as pasta, potatoes, and bread are carbohydrates. They should make up about one third of our diet.

Fruit and Vegetables: The greatest proportion of our diet should be made up of this food group. We should aim to eat at least five portions per day. Fruit and vegetables are a good source of vitamins, minerals, and fiber.

Using the information you have read, label these pictures
with the name of the food group they represent.

Make sure you read
the information on
the left if you are
struggling!

Milkshake mayhem

Color in all the numbered spaces using the key. How many milkshakes can you find? Write the number below.

How many milkshakes can you find? Write the number here. _ _ _ _ _ _ _ _ _ _

RECIPE TIME!

Rachel is busy baking bread. Can you help her by putting these eight steps in the recipe into the right order? Write "1" next to the first step, "2" next to the second step, and so on.

The first one has been done for you.

1 Gather all the ingredients

☐ Put the bread in the oven to cook

☐ Knead the dough

☐ Leave the dough to rise

☐ Mix the ingredients

☐ Weigh the correct amount of each ingredient

NATIONAL CUISINE

Some countries have their very own national dish that forms part of their identity. Match the dish to the country. Use the clues to help you, as some of them you might not have heard of before!

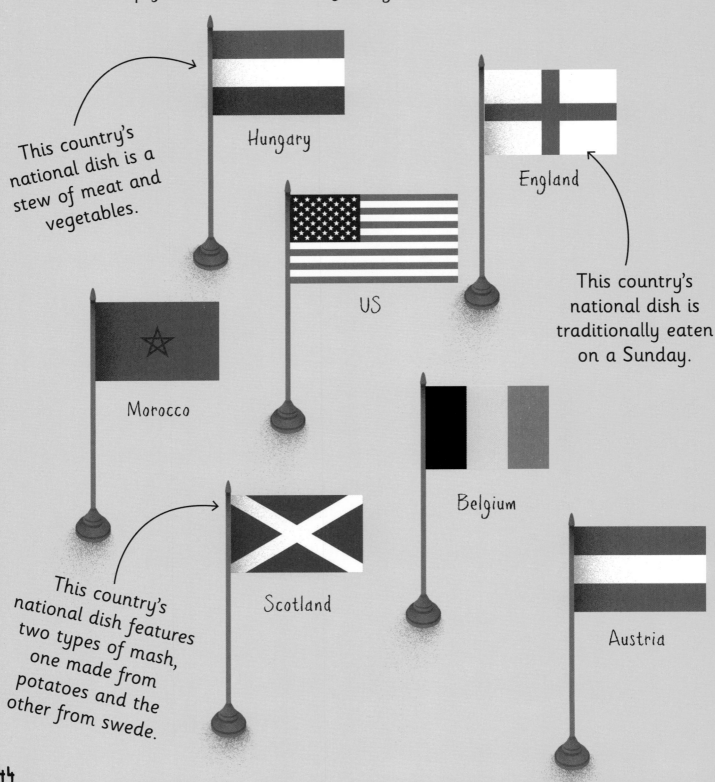

This country's national dish is a stew of meat and vegetables.

Hungary

England

US

This country's national dish is traditionally eaten on a Sunday.

Morocco

Belgium

Scotland

This country's national dish features two types of mash, one made from potatoes and the other from swede.

Austria

Roast Beef

Hamburger

Wiener Schnitzel

Goulash

Mussels and fries

This country's flag has yellow on it!

Cous Cous

Haggis

45

Drawing lesson

Copy the picture of The Coffee Club below onto the
grid on the right. Part of it has been started for you.
Draw it square by square, using the numbers as a guide.
Once you have finished, color in your picture.

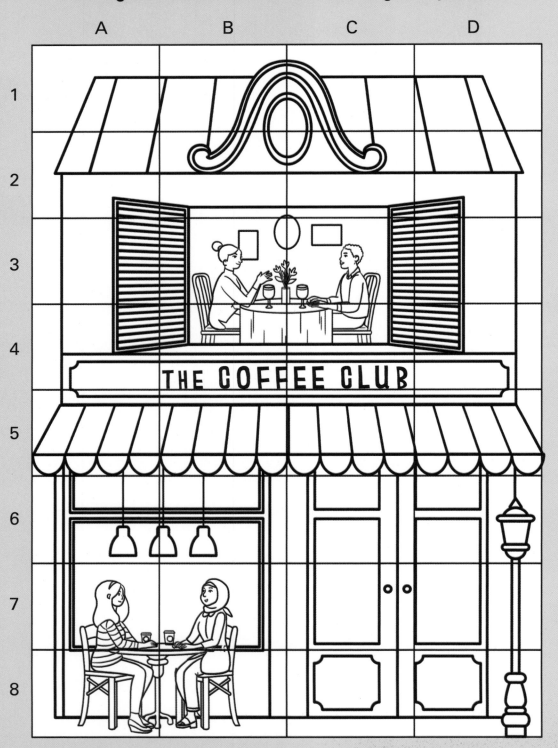

THE COFFEE CLUB

	A	B	C	D
1				
2				
3				
4				
5				
6				
7				
8				

Shapes and cakes

How many rectangles, triangles, and circles can you spot in the cakes below? Write your answers in the boxes below.

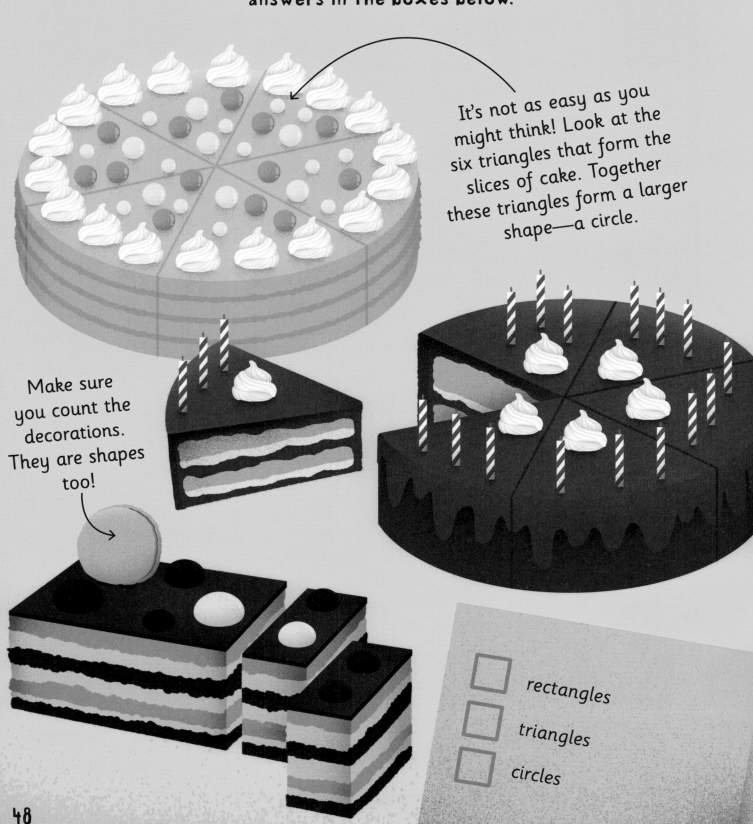

It's not as easy as you might think! Look at the six triangles that form the slices of cake. Together these triangles form a larger shape—a circle.

Make sure you count the decorations. They are shapes too!

☐ rectangles

☐ triangles

☐ circles

Wordsearch

Find the different types of fruit in the wordsearch puzzle below. The words may be forward, backward, up, down, or diagonal. Circle the words as you find them.

Pears ripen best off the tree.

Lemons have a sour taste because they contain citric acid.

A peach is a type of drupe, a fruit with a central stone or seed.

Oranges are hybrids of pomelos and mandarins.

I	L	V	L	E	M	O	N
A	W	R	M	C	L	I	A
M	E	I	Q	A	A	M	F
X	E	L	K	V	N	P	G
D	J	L	P	K	A	G	G
V	H	M	O	P	N	V	O
R	B	O	I	N	A	H	Q
E	L	V	M	Y	B	O	E

There are thousands of different varieties of apple grown around the world.

1. Melon 2. Apple
3. Banana 4. Kiwi
5. Mango 6. Lemon

FOOD JOURNEYS: FROM FARM TO TABLE

It takes lots of different people to get a delicious dinner served to you at your table. Shall we have a look and see how your food got here?

1. Your food starts off at a farm where it is grown or produced. At arable farms, vegetables and crops are grown. At pastoral farms, animals and animal products are farmed.

2. Your food is then processed and packaged so it is ready for the supermarket or to be used in a restaurant.

3. The next step is distribution. The food is transported from the factory to the restaurant or store.

4. Now at the restaurant, your food is prepared and cooked ready for you to eat!

The distance from where something is grown to where it is eaten is the food miles for that product. Because food is transported by boats, planes, and cars, higher food miles mean certain foods have a high carbon footprint. Eating foods with lower food miles reduces pollution and protects the planet.

Use your math skills to fill in the missing food miles for the below products.

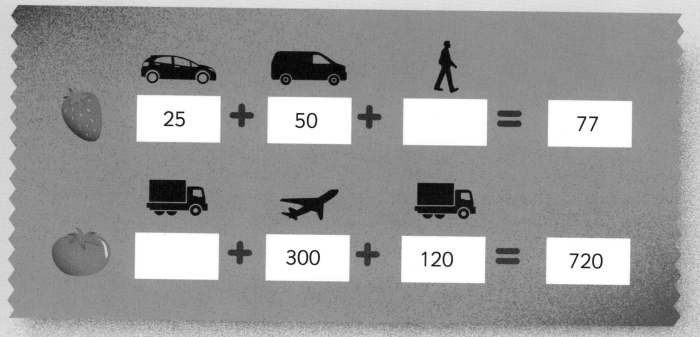

25 + 50 + ___ = 77

___ + 300 + 120 = 720

color it in

This scene needs your coloring skills to make it burst
with bright colors. Use pencils, crayons, or felt tips.

SUNDAE CENTRAL

Check, please!

Jenny is in the food hall having her lunch. She spent $10 on her meal. These five different lunches add up to different amounts. Use your math skills to add up the prices and find out what Jenny ordered for lunch.

Meal 1

$5
$3
$1

Total:........

Meal 2

$5
$2
$3

Total:........

Meal 3

$2
$2
$5

Total:........

Meal 4

$2
$3
$2
$1

Total:........

Meal 5

$1
$5
$2

Total:........

What meal did Jenny have for lunch?

....

COOKERY COMPETITION

Yasmin is taking part in a cookery competition this evening. She is in the running for the Chef's Hat Best Cook Award. Can you help her by circling the ingredients she needs in the fridge and on the worktop? What do you think Yasmin is cooking?

1. spaghetti   4. garlic
2. tomatoes   5. basil
3. onion   6. burger
                       7. cheese

Maze

You need to make your way around the busy restaurant to give a guest their dinner. There are tables and obstacles everywhere! Can you find your way through this maze to the hungry customer?

SPECIALS

Roast Lamb

Vegetable Tagine

Salmon Ravioli

MY MEAL AT THE RESTAURANT

Fill in this keepsake diary of your time at the restaurant. It can be real or imaginary!

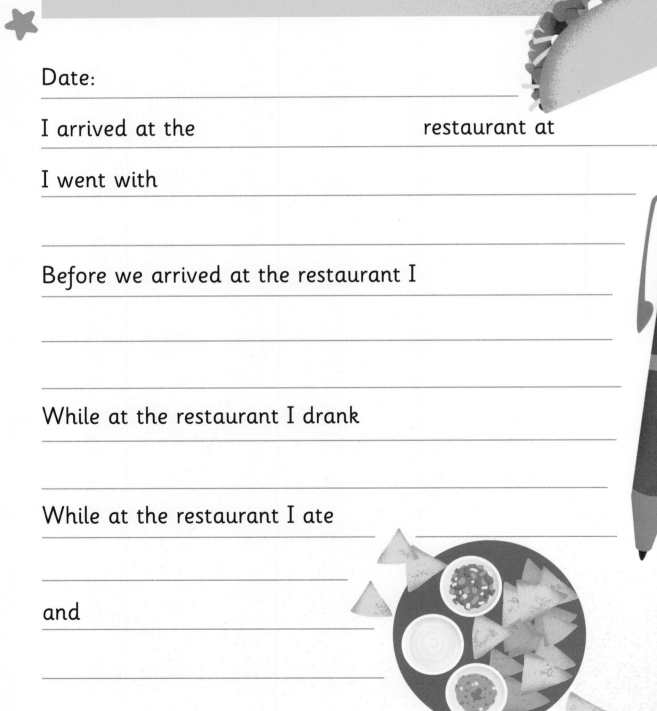

Date:

I arrived at the _____ restaurant at

I went with

Before we arrived at the restaurant I

While at the restaurant I drank

While at the restaurant I ate

and

My favorite part of the meal was

_____

_____

Next time I would order

_____

_____

While at the restaurant I noticed

_____

and

_____

_____

The first thing I will do after the meal will be

_____

_____

The next restaurant I go to will be

_____

in space/under the sea/on a mountain (circle your choice)

_____

and I will eat...

_____

_____

Now, draw your next
restaurant trip in the
space provided.

ANSWERS

PAGE 6: WHO'S THE CHEF?

PAGE 9: DOT-TO-DOT

PAGE 10: SUPERFOODS—TRUE OR FALSE?

1. False
2. True
3. True
4. True
5. False
6. False

PAGE 12: NUMBER SEARCH

9	6	6	8	7	7	9	4
4	3	4	5	6	4	7	9
8	7	5	8	1	3	4	9
3	7	6	8	9	2	1	6
6	8	4	2	3	4	2	5
9	3	5	5	3	6	7	2
4	0	2	5	8	7	6	9
1	7	0	3	9	6	8	6

PAGE 13: I SPY GAME

PAGE 14: GUESS WHO?

PAGE 18: SHADOW MATCH

1. Ice cream
2. French fries
3. Donut
4. Cake
5. Banana
6. Apple

PAGE 19: UNTANGLE A MAZE OF MESSY SPAGHETTI

PAGE 20: SPOT THE DIFFERENCE

PAGE 24: CAN YOU FIND?

PAGE 30: WHAT'S WRONG?

PAGE 32: GOOD SERVICE

1. Green
2. Orange juice
3. A banana skin
4. Six
5. Blonde
6. Three
7. Salad

PAGE 36: AWARE OF THE ALLERGENS!

3	1	2	4
4	2	1	3
2	4	3	1
1	3	4	2

PAGE 37: PICNIC IN THE PARK

PAGE 40: HEALTHY EATING

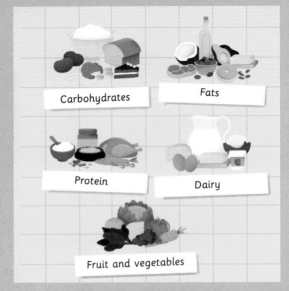

PAGE 42: MILKSHAKE MAYHEM

PAGE 44: NATIONAL CUISINE

1. Hungary——Goulash
2. England——Roast Beef
3. USA——Hamburger
4. Morocco——Cous Cous
5. Belgium——Mussels and fries
6. Scotland——Haggis
7. Austria——Wiener Schnitzel

PAGE 48: SHAPES AND CAKES

1. 21 rectangles
2. 36 triangles
3. 43 circles

PAGE 49: WORDSEARCH

I	L	V	L	E	M	O	N
A	W	R	M	C	L	I	A
M	E	I	Q	A	A	M	F
X	E	L	K	V	N	P	G
D	J	L	P	K	A	G	G
V	H	M	O	P	N	V	O
R	B	O	I	N	A	H	Q
E	L	V	M	Y	B	O	E

PAGE 50: FOOD JOURNEYS: FROM FARM TO TABLE

strawberry: 25 + 50 + 2 = 77 miles
tomato: 300 + 300 + 120 = 720 miles

PAGE 54: CHECK, PLEASE!

Meal 2: Dahl ($5) + naan ($3) + tea ($2) = $10

PAGE 55: COOKERY COMPETITION

She is cooking spaghetti bolognese

PAGE 56: MAZE

Brimming with creative inspiration, how-to projects, and useful information to enrich your everyday life, quarto.com is a favourite destination for those pursuing their interests and passions.

Words by Alice Hobbs
Illustrations by Putri Febriana

Editorial Assistant: Alice Hobbs
Designer: Kevin Knight
Art Director: Susi Martin
Publisher: Holly Willsher

First published in 2022 by QEB Publishing,
an imprint of The Quarto Group.
100 Cummings Center,
Suite 265D Beverly, MA 01915, USA.
T (978) 282-9590 F (978) 283-2742
www.quarto.com

A CIP record for this book is available from the Library of Congress.

ISBN: 978-0-7112-7550-8

9 8 7 6 5 4 3 2 1

Manufactured in Huizhou City, Guangdong, China TT032022

Why not try these other activity books?

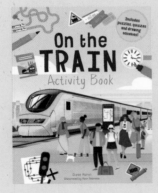

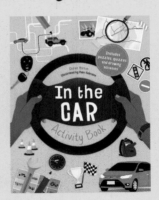